College Application Essay Tips

Do's and Don'ts for a Powerful and Convincing
Admissions Essay

Linda Chiara

Dear Student,

I'm so delighted that you selected this handbook to help guide you through the complexities of writing a compelling college application essay.

The book will delve into the essential stages of essay writing, including brainstorming, outlining, and drafting, while giving you practical tips and tricks to help you overcome writer's block and craft an engaging essay. It also includes inspiring examples of successful essays from real students, as well as expert tips and advice on common pitfalls to avoid. I'll cover all the do's and don'ts in full detail.

Whether you're a high school student just starting the college search process, or a senior polishing your final draft, this practical handbook was designed to help you secure your place at the school of your choice. Sharing your experience with a positive review would be greatly appreciated!

Contents

Chapter One

Introduction: What You Need to Know First

One – one thousand,
Two – one thousand,
Three – one thou…….that's it!

That's all the time you have to impress this admissions officer.

Not even a full three seconds. Amazing, isn't it? I'll explain in a moment why that is, but for now what you need to know is this:

> **When you write your college essay you need to GRAB the reader's ATTENTION in your opening line, right out of the gate.**

It took this admissions officer less than three seconds to put down your essay and place it on top of the dreadful rejection pile before moving on to the next.

Could it be that you simply caught this official on a bad day?

Or is it that perhaps she is incapable of instantly recognizing a masterpiece when she sees one?

Hmm, probably not the reason. You might have had a good enough application essay, but it might not be good enough. The most likely scenario is that this officer has a truck load of application essays waiting to be read. She's already poured through several hundred essays since the application season began and still has hundreds more to go. So don't be surprised to learn that she has a remarkably short attention span. Any college admissions officer will zip through the first paragraph of your page at supersonic speed. If you can't catch her attention quick enough, you're doomed.

It's not sufficient to write an average college essay. Nor is it enough to write a good essay, particularly if you're aiming for a competitive school. Instead, what you need to write is an EXCEPTIONAL college essay. One so honest, well-written, and heart-felt that it knocks the socks off of them.

And the most challenging part is that you only get a few seconds to demonstrate that your work is worth reading all the way through.

You'd be surprised to learn how many applicant students are clueless about this. Understanding this concept will put you in a great position as you craft your essay.

Okay, That's Fine. But What's the Secret Ingredient to Writing an Exceptional College App Essay? Especially If You're Not Particularly a Creative Writer.

The secret ingredient is simply to make an emotional connection and move your reader in some way. Of course, your essay must be impressive and well-developed, but most of all it must do its job.

What is its job?

Its job is to reveal aspects of your character and personality that would normally not be exposed in your application package. It should represent you in the best light to a complete stranger. The admissions officer, who as they read your essay, will be picturing in his or her mind what sort of person you are and how you will fit in the school. Someone with the power of making a snap decision that can determine whether or not you get into the school of your dreams.

So how do you write an exceptional, attention-grabbing essay that meets all of this criteria above? You do it by **turning this stranger into a friendly acquaintance.** This should be the <u>focus of your essay</u>. You should be writing your personal essay as if you were speaking to a person whom you're hoping will get to know you better.

Bring a smile, a laugh, or a hint of a tear to their face. This should be your objective; and the best part is that you can do this without being a natural born writer. You just need to do a bit of soul-searching, follow some guidelines and apply good writing techniques and tips you will learn right from this book.

$$***$$

So before I continue get down to the nitty gritty of the details, here are eight important tips you need to follow right from the onset when writing your essay:

1. Start Early if Possible
A great time to start working on writing your essay is some-time in the summer between the end of your junior and beginning of your senior year in high school. Use your free time to think about topics and test out your essay ideas informally with people you trust.

2. Be Honest, Be Yourself
Choose a topic you'd like to write about and use it to show the admissions officer who you are. Don't write what you think they want to hear, because it won't sound sincere. Instead, write about something that you care about and show how it has impacted you. You want to establish an emotional connection with the reader, but without confusing them with your buddy or a therapist.

3. Choose a Narrow Theme that had Significance in Your Life

Many applicants feel they must choose a scholarly topic or a world-shattering event to be able to demonstrate their intellectual prowess. This is a mistake. The admissions officer doesn't want a lesson in history or social economics. Instead, he wants to learn about YOU as a person. You'll have lots of opportunities during your application to demonstrate your academic qualifications, but not during your personal essay. This is your chance to introduce the person behind the school grades and SAT scores and show your delightful personality. A subject as simple as a memorable family vacation can do the trick. Remember, if you have a unique and insightful approach to a plain and ordinary experience, then you have the topic for college you need and the formula for a winning essay.

4. Avoid Negativity

Never, never, never be critical. Never whine. Never be negative. Even if writing about something sad or traumatic, always remain positive. Your essay must end in an upbeat tone.

5. Avoid Polarizing Topics

There are a million things you can write about in your personal essay. From how you enjoy walking in the rain to how you like singing in the shower. But there are two topics you should avoid: religion and politics. Write about either of these topics and you'll be on a certain path to self-destruction. Simply avoid any incendiary topic.

6. Don't Write About Past Illegal Activities

If you used to be a drug addict, served jail time, were caught drinking and driving, or were involved in any other sort of reckless behavior, keep it to yourself. It doesn't matter if you are completely reformed and/or born again. Don't bring it up. It's too risky and will hurt your chances.

7. Proofread Your Essay

You might think this is obvious, but it's such a critical element that it is worth mentioning and repeating: always proofread your essay. Also, make sure to read your essay out loud or have someone else read it out loud to you. This way you can be sure it flows well and sounds conversational.

8. Write and Rewrite

Did you know that Ernest Hemingway rewrote the last page of <u>Farewell to Arms</u> 39 times before he was satisfied?

If you can write your entire essay in one single shot without a rewrite, then you are nothing short of an absolute genius! The reality is that whether it was Ernest Hemingway, John Steinbeck, or any other great American author, they never finished their work on the first try. You write, you rewrite. And then you do it again. That's how it's done.

Let's get started...

Chapter Two

What Should You Write About?

Choosing your application essay topic usually causes a degree of anxiety. You struggle to come up with the right essay idea, but it's not that easy. To compound the problem, colleges aren't much help since they often pose only generic questions, leaving the part of conceiving something creative and clever up to you. So when it's time to select topics to write about for college, you'll need to fire up your brain cells.

However, before you do some serious brain crunching, know this: **it's not a term paper.** So it shouldn't feel like a term paper, nor read like one. The college essay is written for a different audience and a different purpose.

Many students make the mistake of searching for a scholarly, all-engaging topic that's more suited for a term paper than a personal essay. While a good research or term paper is supposed to demonstrate your mastery of a particular academic subject, an admissions essay or personal statement is supposed to reveal the kind of person you are and eventually hope to become.

In the next chapter we're going to review several essay topic ideas and writing prompts. But before we discuss actual topics, you should be clear on what's expected of you through your writing, regardless of the topic you end up choosing. Here's what you need to remember:

Your essay is to help the admissions committee learn about YOU as a person. Why? Because they want to judge whether you will be a good fit for their school.

They want to be sure you'll add quality to the student body through participation and input in student activities. They already know all about your grades and test scores. They might even know you play an instrument or do volunteer work in your community.

But what they need now is to fill the gap with some information that might be missing. Namely, understanding how you interact with the world around you. The way you express yourself. So think of your essay as a means to an end. The end – your goal – is to show the special qualities and characteristics you possess. And you will reach your goal if you leave a memorable impression on the reader's mind.

Ideally, after reading your personal essay, the admissions officer would say to himself *"...what a nice kid; I'd like to have him in the school."*

So now that you understand that the admissions staff wants

to learn things that do not appear in your application package, think of your essay as your golden opportunity to shine. This is a chance to reveal yourself as a unique individual through a story. And don't think for one second that you are not unique! People are like raindrops; there are many, but there are never two exactly the same.

Finally, here are some important "do's" and "don'ts" before you choose your topic:

DO convey an overall positive message. Sarcasm and cynicism don't show your best side.

DON'T let others – your friends or your parents -decide what to write. While it's perfectly fine to brainstorm with them and help you come up with ideas, YOU are the final decision maker.

DO be sincere no matter what your topic is. Whether you choose to write about a personal possession you have grown irrationally attached to, or about how an overseas trip enhanced your cultural awareness, write with your heart.

DON'T use the essay to oversell yourself. This is not a forum for you to show how smart and clever you are. The reader is not interested in your brilliant solutions on how to solve the world's problems. While you can use the essay to pose thoughtful questions, don't try to tell the reader what the answers to the global problems are. They will not be impressed.

DO write about a topic you believe in and feel strongly about.

DON'T overuse imagery. Though imagery should definitely be incorporated into your work, especially as you relate to the reader the full scope of the experience when describing sounds, or sights, or smells, you don't want to abuse it. Otherwise, it will look like you're trying too hard to be creative.

DO focus on only one general theme or idea, rather than trying to cover a complete subject. For example, if you were writing about a trip to another country, the trip itself would be the subject of your essay, but a specific theme within the subject could be how in this trip you fell in love with the food or how a particular set of customs impressed you, or how the trip taught you to understand people from other cultures.

DON'T write anything that might embarrass the reader or make them feel uncomfortable. As I mentioned earlier, stay away from topics involving religion or politics. And if you write about a sensitive topic involving drug abuse, sexuality, etc., be sure to handle it carefully because you'll be walking a tightrope. It's best to avoid cringe worthy subjects in general.

DO write about something you observed and experienced firsthand. Avoid a theme based on secondhand information. Remember, the essay is a personal account of something that happened to YOU.

DON'T write about or mention popular TV shows, musicians, actors or movies. Your admissions officer will not be impressed.

DO be genuine and honest. If you try to portray yourself with values or interests that aren't really yours, your essay will sound fake.

DON'T hire a writing service from a website to write it for you or resort to artificial intelligence. I can guarantee it will lack individuality and sound like so many other essays. Only you can write about what it felt like the first time you rode a bike, or about a family trip to the countryside, or about how your Uncle Charlie once saved a dog's life and the impact it had on you...only you!

Chapter Three

List of Great Essay Topics

Here's a list of essay topics to assist you in your search. Though some schools might propose one for you, e.g. *Explain Why You Chose This School,* there will be other times when they'll allow you to write freely on a subject of your choice. Regardless of the topic you choose, always use an informal, conversational tone in your essay, but make sure it's not as informal as colloquial speech.

This list should give you some great ideas.

The first time you cooked a meal or baked a cake.
Maybe it turned out to be such a great meal it surprised even you, or maybe it turned out to be the most inedible meal ever. Either way, it could make a good story.

A fun or memorable family vacation.
Don't think that a great topic needs to be about a world-consuming event. A simple run-of-the-mill theme like a family trip to the beach could set the stage for a marvelous essay.

One of the most difficult or hardest thing you've ever had to face.

This is a great topic, but be sure not to whine. Nobody likes a whiner.

Loss of someone or something important.

If you choose this topic, you need to demonstrate how the experience made you grow or change in a POSITIVE way.

A memorable work experience.

It could be a team project that went exceptionally well, a rewarding accomplishment such as receiving recognition or a promotion, or even a meaningful interaction with a colleague or manager.

How would your friends describe you?

Make a list of adjectives (see chapter 14) that describe you – i.e. friendly, stubborn, etc. – and think of personal stories or anecdotes where these characteristics showed up.

Of the seven dwarfs from Disney's Snow White, I identify most with...

It's fine to use a bit of humor as long as you don't overdo it. If you incorporate your sense of humor into your essay, remember that an essay filled with puns or off-color jokes is destined to fail.

Volunteer work in your community.

You might have already covered this in your application, so if you choose this one make sure to approach it from an interesting angle.

Moving.
Moving is considered one of the most stressful situations for any family. Can you think of something amusing or entertaining that happened while moving that started out disastrously, but ended up working out well?

The best advice you've ever given someone.
Or a twist to this could be: What advice would you give today to the 12-year old you?

A special teacher that truly inspired you.
Make sure to give examples of how and why.

A day that started out being one of the worst days of your life and ended being one of the best.
Did you ever have one of those days? A day which started terribly, but changed due to the kindness of others, or a change in your perspective, or, perhaps, discovering a solution to a problem. These types of days remind us to stay positive and have hope even in tough situations.

A charismatic or interesting relative or family background.
Is there any member of your family with an interesting hobby or a magnetic personality? Does your family history include a diverse cultural heritage, a notable ancestral history, or overcoming significant challenges or obstacles? Write about it.

A foreign country you visited and how you gained from the experience.
If you choose this one, beware of overdramatizing it. A trip to a third-world country can turn you into a better person;

however you won't come across as authentic unless you are able to support this claim with real believable examples.

A book which had a great impact on your life.
Did you ever read a book that affected you so much it stayed with you for days? A book that you told everyone you knew that they should read it too? Write about that book.

Your first day at school.
Many people have fond memories of their first day of school. Perhaps something that left an indelible impression on your young mind. Or maybe you moved in from another town or school district and have a story to tell.

A character-building challenge or fear you overcame.
Fear of public speaking? Skydiving? Going to the dentist? We all have a fear or phobia of some kind. Tell us how you overcame yours.

A family tradition.
Maybe you decorate the Christmas tree together or go hiking as a family every year to the same place. Think of any family ritual that you found to be bonding through your growing up years.

What was your happiest moment or greatest thrill?
Any single event that stands out?

The best advice you ever received in high school and how it helped you.
Was it from a friend, a teacher, a counselor? How did it impact your life?

A story of when you learned how to drive or when you took your driver's test.

Lots of possibilities here, especially if you had an entertaining adventure.

A story of when you first learned to ride a bicycle.

You can use this same theme by substituting the subject to suit your needs. For example: a story of when you first learned to play tennis, or play guitar, or scuba dive, etc.

One lesson you learned the hard way.

Often when you learn a lesson the hard way, it results in deeper understanding and long-term personal growth. It could be about the negative consequences of procrastinating, the importance of saving money, the value of honesty, etc.

A quote you absolutely love.

You can demonstrate how you've been inspired by that quote and/or how it has been a constant motivating factor in your life.

Someone you have lost contact with that you would really love to talk to.

Is there someone with whom you once had a close relationship and lost touch due to changes in circumstances or life events?

Write about your interest in traveling someday.

Where, when, why, how and with whom?

An essay about a childhood book that changed your life and still has an impact on you today.

Mine was an ordinary book entitled <u>Nurses Who Led the Way.</u> After reading it, I did not necessarily want to become a nurse. Instead, it influenced me to become a writer.

Tell us about a time you stepped out of your comfort zone.
How did the experience help you grow? What did you learn from it? Would you do it again?

Three things you wished you had learned earlier in your life and why.
It doesn't have to be three, it could be one or two things. Anything beyond three becomes a list.

Bottom line, your essay is a small window into a slice of your life, where the reader has the chance to discover interesting aspects of your personality. Any personal experience you've had may end up being the fuel you need to fire up your essay. So dig deep enough inside of you and you'll find your story. I guarantee it!

Chapter Four

Planning Your Essay

When planning an essay, it often helps to choose a title. Though not necessary, a flashy title or a title that gives the reader a hint of what your essay is about, could help, unless you're answering a question that was already posed to you, such as "Why do you wish to attend this university?".

In fact, coming up with an imaginative or creative title can jump start your essay, because it can establish a story and provide you with direction. If you can't decide on a title, don't worry. Often the title comes to you after the essay is written. The important thing is to begin writing.

Laying Down the Foundation

Does your mind feel as blank as your sheet of paper right now?

It's okay. It's perfectly normal. Even the most proficient and well-known authors could teach a master class on procrastination when it comes to actually sitting down and writing. Try this: jot down whatever comes to mind on a few separate sheets of paper.

Don't worry about tying anything together yet. Just as with the production of a Hollywood movie, where the shots are rarely filmed in sequence, this is the production part of your essay where you're simply jotting down random thoughts and observations. The goal is to get your creative juices flowing and generating ideas.

From these ideas, you'll gather enough material to start the first draft of your masterpiece. If you're having trouble working up to this stage, do this: open the list of adjectives (from chapter 13) and identify some of those words that describe you best.

Once you decide on a word, reflect back on any experience, problem, achievement or a topic that you might like to share. For instance, suppose the word *innovative* describes you well. Reflect back on possible topics where being an innovative person became evident. Maybe it got you out of a jam, or maybe you were able to come to the aid of a friend in a time of need. The possibilities are endless.

What Tone Should You Use in Your Essay?

Your essay can be emotional, serious, entertaining, funny, creative or even philosophical. Any type will work, as long as it's written in an honest tone and helps reveal your personality.

1. Your tone should be friendly, confident and assertive. You're proud of your achievements and there's nothing wrong with acknowledging them. But don't over-

do it with self compliments. Don't turn your essay into commercial promoting all your wonderful accomplishments. You should balance your pride with humility, self-evaluation and a generous spirit. Remember, nobody likes a bragger.

2. As a reminder, avoid any sort of whining. Don't try to explain your low test scores by claiming you've been victimized by an unjust system and a cruel world. It will get you nowhere.

3. Don't write it in a formal tone as if it were a research paper. Use an informal and conversational style for your essay, but not as informal as colloquial speech. (*You know, don't like tell us you like to go to Starbucks because it's like your favorite thing.*)

4. Avoid using slang or popular buzz words, unless they're used as part of a dialogue.

Should You Use Humor?

Oh, so you're a funny guy, huh? If you have a lively sense of humor and can't help incorporating it into your writing, it's okay. A touch of humor is fine, as long as it's not overdone. But be extra careful; an essay filled with bad puns or off-color jokes won't make it past the first sentence. If you use humor you've got to make sure that it's not only light and entertaining, but that it's helping you get your point across and saying something important about your experience.

Below is an example of someone who didn't understand the difference between being funny and being dismissive.

The college asked for A Personal Satisfying Experience. This was his response:

"After struggling for what seems like an eternity with this question, I still can't come up with a personally satisfying answer. So, knowing how stressed out you all are this time of year, I've decided to spare you from yet another tedious application essay. I'll simply tell you that I would love to attend your college, and I know that once you get to know me you'll love to have me. Have fun with the rest of your essays!"

Trying to be cute only earned this applicant a not-so-funny rejection letter.

Chapter Five

The Opening Paragraph

Okay, you have your topic selected. The moment of truth is here. Now is the time to put your mind to work and start writing your essay. And it all begins with your opening paragraph.

To fully understand the importance of your opening paragraph, think of your entire essay as a symphony orchestra, where each part of the whole essay plays an important individual role in a team performance. In a symphony orchestra, if one of the violinists hits a bad note, it won't ruin the concert. Perhaps no one even notices. But if the lead violinist stumbles during her solo performance, it'll be in the newspapers the next day.

Though I'm exaggerating about the newspapers obviously (it's called artistic freedom), I'm not kidding when I tell you that the opening paragraph of an essay can make or break it. It has a monumental job: **to grab the reader by the collar and not let him go!** And you've got to do it quickly. It's possible to escape a tragic fate with a weak paragraph in some other part of your essay, but you will never survive a weak opening.

Never underestimate the power of the opening paragraph.

Spend as much time as you need on creating and writing an intro paragraph. But don't despair because usually whatever you write as your essay's opening paragraph, it will rarely end up in your final version. You'll likely go through several drafts, tweaking and editing, particularly as you advance your story.

Start With a Format

Decide on a format for your opening paragraph. You want to generate interest and capture the admissions officer's attention so he stays glued to his seat. You can do this by using one of these following techniques:

1. **Create a Feeling of Mystery or Intrigue**
   Intro Paragraph Example:
   "With only a few coins left in my pocket and a broken heart, I gathered my belongings and reluctantly walked down the stairway."

Anyone reading a first paragraph such as this would surely feel compelled to continue reading, so he can find out why you're sad, reluctant, and broke. You've got him "hooked."

2. **Fact or Statement**
Start out with a startling fact, an anecdote, or a statement or description about yourself.

Intro Paragraph Example:
"Roses make a wonderful addition to my grandmother's garden, but they need a lot of water. Sometimes I feel like a rose, soaking up the world around me, eager to flourish and bloom."

Another Example:
"Over seventy-percent of Americans have a terrifying fear of public speaking, so I knew I wasn't alone; but I also knew it was time for me to conquer these jitters."

In their own particular way, both paragraphs begin from a general fact or statistic, only to swiftly personalize the statement and invite the reader to learn more about the author.

3. **Dialogue**
Start with a line of dialogue. This is usually a reliable opening, because the reader quickly tunes into your voice and tone. To apply this technique effectively, you need to Identify the speaker, identify the place, and use quotes.

Intro Paragraph Example:
"Mom, phone! It's for you." My twelve-year-old voice rang out nervously across the hallway of our small, but comfortable New York apartment. Standing by the oven in the kitchen, my mom couldn't hide the annoyed look on her face as she shouted, "Whoever it is, tell them I'll call them back later." I felt instant relief, as the caller was none other than my homeroom teacher!"

The format above consists of: — Quote / First Speaker Identification / Place Description — Second Speaker Identification / Quote — Back to First Speaker.

Of course, you can vary the format to suit your purpose. For instance: Place Description / Speaker Identification / Quote, as illustrated below:

"As the phone rang, I raced down the hallway of our New York apartment with my heart pounding. "Mom, phone! It's for you," my trembling twelve-year old voice shouted."

And although dialogue is a great way to go, it's not the only way.

Courtesy of Stanford University, here are ten opening lines from previous Stanford admission essays, all from students who were accepted into the university. Each opening line is enticing, and enough to make the reader want to continue reading:

- I change my name each time I place an order at Starbucks.

- When I was in the eighth grade I couldn't read.

- While traveling through the daily path of life, have you ever stumbled upon a hidden pocket of the universe?

- I have old hands.

- I was paralyzed from the waist down. I would try to move my leg or even shift an ankle but I never got a response. This was the first time thoughts of death ever cross my mind.

- I almost didn't live through September 11th, 2001.

- The spaghetti burbled and slushed around the pan, and as I stirred it, the noises it gave off began to sound increasingly like bodily functions.

- I have been surfing Lake Michigan since I was three years old.

- I stand on the riverbank surveying this rippled range like some riparian cowboy -instead of chaps, I wear vinyl, thigh-high waders and a lasso of measuring tape and twine is slung over my arm.

- I had never seen anyone get so excited about mitochondria.

***

Here are some important "<u>don'ts</u>" to keep in mind as you work through your introductory paragraph:

- **Don't** underestimate the importance of a great opening paragraph.

- **Don't** get caught up in the "big word" frenzy. It's not about big words, it's about big ideas.
  "I don't mean to sound invidious, but this essay tutorial has sonorously left me in a state of ennui." —- Huh? What? Say that again? In truth, this sort of writing won't even serve you well in an English composition, let alone a college application essay. While a thesaurus is a handy companion, great ideas are often expressed in the simplest language.

- **Don't** summarize your entire essay in your first paragraph. Remember, you're trying to keep the reader intrigued enough to read the full essay.

- **Don't** use fluff expressions that fail to add value to your sentence structure. Instead be efficient with your choice of words. For example, don't say *"At that point in time"*, when instead you can simply say "Then". (Review expressions to avoid in your essay in chapter 13).

I've underscored the importance of the starting paragraph. To help you along, see the next chapter on *Opening Paragraph Techniques*. Don't worry if after many attempts you still can't seem to come up with the perfect opening. Remember, this is only your first draft! You can always come back and improve your opening later.

Chapter Six

Fifteen Opening Paragraph Techniques

In our previous chapter I explained how the opening paragraph's job is to grab the reader's attention.

One approach you might find helpful, is to think of your reader as someone who is only half awake as they're about to read your essay. Consider how you would like to immediately wake them up and focus on you in a positive way.

Here are opening paragraph techniques to contemplate as you prepare to write your essay. Some of these intro paragraph examples are from authentic essays, which were written by successful applicants to real colleges (from Peterson's Best College Admission Essays). Of course, like all examples in this book, they are just meant for demonstration and clarification, not to be copied and pasted in your own essay. But hopefully they serve for sparking your imagination!

***

1. Begin your essay with an intriguing statement that makes your readers wonder to whom or to what you are referring:

I had a mental image of them standing there, wearing ragged clothes, hot and depressed, looking upon us as intruders in their world. We would invade their territory only to take pictures and observe them like tourists.

2. Make a reference to a familiar occasion. Readers pay attention when you mention an occasion or incident they recognize:

For most of my life, Veteran's Day has meant little more than parades, flags, and a day off school. But this year my attitude has taken a more serious tone as a result of a course I took on modern warfare.

3. Start with a personal anecdote:

I remember the day my grandmother gifted me a sketchbook and a set of pencils. I didn't know it then, but that simple gesture sparked a lifelong passion for drawing and painting.

4. Use a metaphor:

I see my life as a puzzle, with each experience adding a new piece. Attending your college will complete the puzzle and help me become the person I'm dreaming to be.

5. Start your essay with a confession:

If each person's life could be likened to a book, the early chapters of mine would be some of the fullest. My childhood in Germany and my travels throughout the continent have shaped me in countless ways. I want to share with you one small chapter of my life, which took place in Florence, Italy, where I became acquainted with a man named David.

6. Share a personal story:

I remember the first time I saw the ocean. I was just a child, but the vastness of it took my breath away. From that moment on, I knew that somehow the ocean would be a big part of my life. My goal now is to pursue a degree in marine biology.

7. Begin your essay asking a question to rouse the reader's curiosity. However, be careful. You need to be sure you answer the question(s) in the body of your essay, and also be sure to limit your questions to not more than two or three:

Imagine you're an editor for the high school yearbook and you discover after doing some opinion research that sales are down and student apathy is up. What would you do to increase sales? Would you revamp the format or stick to the traditional approach? How would you get the support of the faculty and the administration on any changes you suggest? These are three questions I had to answer as I worked on the yearbook this fall.

8. Tell a narrative. It should be specific and easy to follow, while creating suspense and leading the reader right into the heart of the subject:

I remember the first time I tried a scientific experiment. The kid next door had one of those do-it-yourself-kits. No one was home and we set up shop. We were too sophisticated to read the manual, so we made our own concoctions using a little of this and a lot of that. We held our secret formula over a flame, bringing it to a boil, and waited and waited – and waited.

9. Start with dialogue or a trivial observation that anyone can relate to but only you can write:

"He looks like Old Man Winter," my friend Mark said, looking at a picture of my grandfather, whose steel-white mustache and thinning around his mostly bald scalp gave off a sense of warm wisdom. In the picture he is holding my two-year old cousin and because of that he smiles in happiness. "Is he the one who takes you skiing?" "Yeah," I answered, "he taught me how to ski."

10. Begin your essay giving facts or details. However, don't overdo it by giving too many facts or details, otherwise the reader may become bored waiting to see how this relates to the main point of your story:

I've always been impressed by people who have made great achievements at an early age. Alexander Hamilton was Lieutenant Colonel at 20, a framer of the US Constitution at 30, and the Secretary of the Treasury at 32. Alexander Graham Bell invented the telephone at 28, and George Eastman produced dry plates for photography at 26. Although my parents and teachers coax me to slow down, I'm eager to make my mark as soon as possible.

11. Compare and contrast two perspectives:

Growing up in a rural area and then moving to a city, I've seen the stark contrast between the two environments. I've learned that each place has its own beauty, and I want to explore these differences further through my college studies.

12. Use a quote:

Steve Jobs once said, "Your work is going to fill a large part of your life, and the only way to be truly satisfied is to do what you believe is great work." This quote has stuck with me as I've grown and developed my passions.

13. Use imagery to create a scene:

The smell of freshly baked cookies filled the air as I stepped into the kitchen. My grandmother was rolling dough, and I knew that this was the moment that I wanted to learn how to make them.

14. Use descriptive language:

The wind was howling, the rain was coming down in sheets, and the waves were crashing against the rocks. But I didn't care. I was in my element.

15. Start with a counter-intuitive statement:

I've always hated math, but it was the one subject that taught me the most about myself.

Before you start writing your essay, review the next chapter so you're familiar with the common essay mistakes you MUST avoid.

Chapter Seven

Eight Common Mistakes You MUST Avoid

Let's review eight common mistakes that many students make. Any one of these below could represent a potential landmine for your essay, so we're going to examine each one carefully with examples and show you how to avoid them. These are the mistakes:

1. Wordiness

2. Vagueness

3. Overuse of "I"

4. Digressing ineffectively

5. Using clichés

6. Overuse of adjectives and adverbs

7. Using the passive voice

8. Lack of focus

Mistake 1: **Wordiness**

Your essay should not be so bland that it's downright boring, but it shouldn't be too wordy either. Take a look at the paragraph below. It's an example of a wordy paragraph. It's full of unnecessary words that are distracting and getting in the way of forward progress. See if you can spot what's wrong:

> *There was no chance on earth that I could have ever imagined myself one day skating so well and confidently in our local neighborhood ice skating rink. The first time I ever went to the rink with my older brother and cousins, and they talked me into skating, I was ten years old and petrified. I remember distinctively feeling like the world was spinning around me, and I watched most of it while on my butt on the rink floor. But now I must say that skating gives me an exhilarating feeling of rush and relaxation all at the same time.*

Before we continue, take a moment on your own and try to eliminate what you believe could be eliminated from the paragraph above.

***

Now let's review...

The sections in bold are the words that can be scaled back or cut out completely:

> ***There was no chance on earth*** *that I could have ever imagined myself one day skating so well and confidently in **our local neighborhood ice skating rink. The first time I ever went to the rink** with my older brother and cousins, and they talked me into skating, I was ten years old and petrified. **I remember distinctively** feeling like the world was spinning around me, and I watched most of it while on my butt on the rink floor. But now **I must say** that skating gives me an exhilarating feeling of rush and relaxation all at the same time.*

Let's break it down:

There was no chance on earth – this type of expression you use in regular speech, but avoid it in your college essay unless it's part of a dialogue.

Neighborhood ice skating rink – there are instances where too much detail gets in the way and even distracts from the story. In this case, neighborhood ice skating rink took the momentum out of the sentence.

The first time I ever went to the rink – not wrong, but not necessary if it's not progressing the story. This is the sort of phrase you would cut out by the second draft of your essay, as you review your final essay for tightness and completeness.

I remember distinctively – same as above.

I must say that – just plain fluff. Always avoid fluff words in your essay. (See chapter 12)

Remember - by your final draft you want your essay to be tight and to be void of unnecessary words.

Mistake 2: **Vagueness**
Can you tell what's wrong with this paragraph?

> *There is so much I enjoy about Christmas. I find a lot of the activities and customs surrounding this holiday so fun and joyful. I hope to have children someday, so I can pass many of these wonderful traditions on to them.*

If you're thinking it's not so terrible of a paragraph, I agree with you. It's not terrible, it's just boring. What makes it so dull is its vagueness.

It's okay to start with a general statement as long as you immediately follow-up with some specifics, which the author failed to do. Without specifics your essay becomes dull and indistinguishable. In this case, the author missed the chance to describe with clarity what she means by "activities and customs". Remember, never miss the chance to paint an image in the reader's mind with a precise description.

Let's rewrite it:

> *There is so much I enjoy about Christmas. From baking cookies and hanging stockings to singing Christmas carols by the fireplace, I find it all fun and joyful. I hope to have children someday, so I can pass these wonderful traditions on to them.*

See the difference visual imagery makes?

Mistake 3: **Overuse of "I"**

> *I always wanted to play the drums since as far back as I can remember. I banged on pots and pans from the age of two, and I begged my parents shamelessly nonstop for a drum set until I finally got my first set at the age of five. I still play them every chance I get. I also learned to play piano as part of the deal I made with my parents for getting my drums, though I never became as proficient on the piano as I am with my beloved drums.*

There are four sentences in the paragraph above and eleven uses of the word "I".

By its own nature, a college personal essay is about YOU. Therefore, it stands to reason that it's written in first-person narrative, posing a challenge for the writer. How do you write about yourself without sounding repetitive and narcissistic with your use of the word "I"? Don't worry, it's something easily correctable with minor sentence restructuring. Usually, you would make these corrections during your second or final draft of your admission essay, as you're reviewing for tightness and completeness.

Let's try rewriting it:

> *Since my early childhood, I've always wanted to play the drums. After banging on pots and pans from the age of two and shamelessly begging my parents nonstop for a drum set, I got my first set by the age of five. To this day, I continue to play the drums in my spare time. I also learned to play piano as part of the agreement with my parents for getting my original drum set, though never becoming as proficient on the piano as I've become with my beloved drums.*

Still four sentences, but down to just five "I"s. Better, wouldn't you agree?

Mistake 4: **Digressing ineffectively**

In the passage below, you'll see in bold how the writer digresses from his main point:

> *Although I wouldn't define it as a character-building undertaking, my time working at Taco Bell was an interesting learning experience.* **In reality, it was a much better experience than several of the other part-time jobs I held during high school.** *Dealing with a range of difficult personalities and demanding customers made me appreciate more the art of politeness and good manners.*

Digressing or deviating from your main point to insert an engaging aside anecdote could be a good thing in your essay, particularly if it enhances the reading experience. But if the side note is pointless and adds no value, as in the case above, then it is only getting in the way from advancing the story. Ask yourself – how would the paragraph look without it?

Let's try it:

> *Although I wouldn't define it as a character-building undertaking, my time working at Taco Bell was an interesting learning experience. Dealing with a range of difficult personalities and demanding customers made me appreciate the often missing art of politeness and good manners.*

It made the paragraph much more fluid giving it forward progression. However, if you still wanted to digress and add an aside, this perhaps would have been a better way:

Although I wouldn't define it as a character-building undertaking, my time working at Taco Bell was an interesting learning experience. In reality, the job provided more than just a means for me to pay my car expenses during high school. It taught me to deal with a range of difficult personalities and demanding customers made me appreciate the often missing art of politeness and good manners.

Mistake 5: **Using clichés**

This student was asked to submit a personal statement describing someone who has been an important influence in his life. See if you can identify the problem with it:

If there's ever been a tried and true person in my life, it's been James. He would always find a way to cheer me up when the chips were down, and never missed the boat when it came to supporting me in any of my highs school endeavors. Whether cheering me on at track and field or helping me overcome my fear of algebra, I knew I could always count on him. By the same token, everyone I know respects and admires James for the person he is. As luck would have it, he's my oldest brother, and I couldn't imagine someone better in my life to emulate.

The problem is that though the snippet above contains some elements of good stylistic writing (i.e. the revelation at the end), it's unfortunately fraught with clichés. A cliché is an over-used and tired phrase. It lacks originality, thereby failing to inspire the reader. And if you can't inspire the admissions committee guess where your admission essay ends up? That's correct, in the recycling bin. Let's not let that happen.

Here's our snippet with the clichés highlighted. Let's see if you've identified the same things that I did:

*If there's ever been a **tried and true** person in my life, it's been James. He would always find a way to cheer me up when **the chips were down**, and never **missed the boat** when it came to supporting me in any of my high school events. Whether cheering me on at track and field or helping me overcome my fear of algebra, I knew I could always count on him. **By the same token**, everyone I know respects and admires James for the person he is. **As luck would have it**, he's my oldest brother, and I couldn't imagine someone better in my life to emulate.*

Though the first use of the cliché – tried and true – would not have been totally offending on its own, it becomes annoying once all the other clichés follow. Here's a better way:

If there's ever been an influential person in my life, it's been James. He would always find a way to cheer me up when I needed it most, and never missed the opportunity to support me through high school. Whether cheering me on at the track and field or helping me overcome my fear of algebra, I knew I could always count on him. Even though everyone respects and admires James for the person he is, I remain his greatest admirer. After all, he's not only one of the most influential people in my life, he's also my oldest brother. I couldn't imagine someone better to emulate.

Mistake 6: **Overuse of adjectives and adverbs**

Excessive use of ornamental language will hurt your college essay. When you find yourself using adjectives and adverbs in practically every sentence, it's time for a rewrite. You'll need to tone it down or your essay will sound too melodramatic, like this one for instance:

*Attending the Seattle Philharmonic's opening night symphony was one of the most **marvelously wonderful** experiences of my life. The way their superstar pianist **nimbly and dexterously** moved his hands through the keyboard, while the cellist reciprocally accompanied every note in a **harmoniously exquis-***

ite *fashion, was* **breathtaking.** *It left me* **desperate-ly** *wanting it to never end.*

When I paint a picture in my mind of what this writer is like, I can't help but think of a puppy dog running all over vying for my attention. The writer tried hard to impress, but he sadly failed. The point this student is trying to make is that he attended Seattle Philharmonic's opening night symphony, the musicians were wonderful and the experience left a lasting impression. But it's difficult to see the message through all the theatrics and overuse of embellishing language. Let's revise it:

> *Attending the Seattle Philharmonic's opening night symphony was one of the most wonderful experiences of my life. Watching their superstar pianist perform while the cellist exquisitely accompanied him was breathtaking. It's an adventure I will never forget.*

Remember, a little ornamental language is GOOD. But a lot is BAD.

Mistake 7: **Using the passive voice**

The passive voice is often necessary, but you need to be mindful of how and when you use it. If you overdo it, you risk your essay becoming wordy and stuffy. Let's analyze this passage:

As the finished line was approached by the leading runners, the roar of the crowd could be heard. If the line wasn't crossed by me first, our chance for Regionals would be lost.

It's clearly a defining moment in the race, but it doesn't feel like it with so much passive voice. Its dramatic edge was lost. This paragraph can clearly be improved. Or, better yet, shall we say let's improve this paragraph.

As I approached the finish line with the leading runners, the roar of the crowd became deafening. I had to cross the line first or our chance for Regionals was lost.

The active voice put the drama back into the race.

Mistake 8: **Lack of focus**

A common mistake students make is failing to address a specific question. For example, if the question is "Why did you choose this college?", you can be assured that they want specifics. Take a look at this snippet below taken from a personal statement addressing the question of why the student wants to attend Occidental College:

I believe Occidental College is an excellent match for me. College should be more than just an entryway to our future careers, but rather a learning ground preparing students in various facets of life, so they are ready for the range of challenges and opportunities that lie ahead. Though I have not yet decided on a major, my inclination is in the liberal arts, where I have excelled in subjects such as English, History, and Political Science, all areas in which Occidental excels. I am an intellectually curious person by nature who loves to read fiction and nonfiction alike. My dream is to influence and positively contribute to the world around me, and I'm convinced Occidental College will provide me that with the broad-based education that will help me reach my dream.

You be the judge. Did this student adequately answer the question? The answer is no. To prove it, replace Occidental College with Amherst College, or CCSU, or St. John's University, or any other school that offers a liberal arts program. It would make no difference; they would all be interchangeable. Why? Because the student simply failed to point the unique attributes that attracted her to Occidental, and unfortunately this is what the college wanted to hear.

If you're faced with a similar question, remember that all it takes is a little bit of online research on your school of choice. Learn some of what the school offers and decide which particular features are right for you.

Chapter Eight

Essay Body: Crafting Your Story

As you develop your essay body paragraph structure, think of the body paragraphs as a means to support your ideas. The body paragraph structure should relate to your introduction, with each paragraph flowing naturally and logically to the next. Therefore, your first challenge with the body is deciding on a suitable style for your admission essay. The most common and easiest style to handle is the chronological style.

The chronological style is an account of the events arranged in order of occurrence. The format you apply to your body paragraph structure will depend on the experience you're relating. Some experiences fall naturally into a past-to-present format, while others may need a present-to-past and back-to-present format. A more difficult style to master is called the experience frame. Here, you're using stream of consciousness, sophisticated transitions, and careful flashing back and forth. It's a more complicated format, and requires very developed writing skills for it to work.

Developing Your Story – First Draft

Have you ever watched a movie that seemed confusing? One where you're watching a scene that doesn't seem related to the scene before it and you feel as if something is missing? Usually, it's the result of a poor editing job between scenes. Your essay is not much different from a movie. Only instead of scenes they're called paragraphs and your job is to seamlessly link them together.

As you develop your story, each paragraph within your body paragraph structure should support the next. From your opening paragraph to your second and each subsequent paragraph, your essay must feel like it's moving forward. This is called **forward progression**. It gives the reader the implicit assurance that there's a point to your story – a beginning, a middle and an end. Even if using a present to past to present format, your story must move forward. How do you do this? First, by having a central theme or a plot (go back to selecting your essay topic if you haven't done this yet).

You need to know how you want to begin your story and where you eventually want to take the reader. But you might not really know this from the onset. It's likely you'll start with one idea, and then as the story unfolds it will take shape and lead you in a different direction. That's fine. That's why it's called a first draft. You write a paragraph or two. Then you go back and tweak them, and then you write some more. And as you're writing and tweaking, your creative juices start rushing like water from a sink as you envision the conclusion.

Show Don't Tell

You may have a constant theme that runs throughout the entire essay. Or you may simply be putting passages together in a logical sequence. Regardless of your approach, you must make sure with each paragraph that you SHOW, not simply TELL, your experience. Here's the difference:

An example of TELL:
I consider myself a highly motivated, talented, and dedicated student. I wasn't always this way, but I've discovered the magical results that one can achieve with a little sacrifice and hard work. They will always go a long way with helping you accomplish your objectives in life. I always work hard to keep my grades up, and to stay physically fit by participating in various varsity sports. I'm proud of the results I've achieved so far. I plan to continue applying myself with the same enthusiasm and dedication, and hope to reach someday, the ambitious career goals I have set for myself." blah blah blah, yada yada yada..

An example of SHOW:
"Runners take your marks," shouts the starter. My heart begins pounding hard, as I crouch down, rub my sweaty hands together, and plant my fingertips on the white line of the pavement. "Get set," yells the man with the gun. My hips shoot up. A burst of

excitement fills my body. My knee is scarred and my shin is bruised from all those practice drills and long hours of hard training, but my will and determination is stronger than ever. I am ready!

"Boom" blasts the gun. As I explode down the lane and approach the first hurdle, I think back to a time when I didn't believe in myself. A time when I didn't understand the value of personal sacrifice and hard work. And now here I am on my way to the finish line. I don't know if I'll be the first one to cross it or not, but it doesn't matter. I'm still excited. Because now I can close my eyes and picture myself crossing any finish line I may face in life."

Which better conveys the value of hard work and dedication? Hopefully, you chose the second. There's a huge difference between these two paragraphs that you need to recognize.

In the TELL paragraph, the writer is simply listing a series of qualities he claims to possess. Since he's not offering any supporting evidence to back up his claims, he expects the reader to just take his word for it.

In the SHOW paragraph, the writer draws us into his story with his tone and voice. He's not expecting us to simply believe him. Instead, he's showing us through his use of imagery. The TELL paragraph falls short of its goal of contributing to a memorable – or at least an interesting – essay. Though the paragraph is grammatically and structurally correct, it's missing the elements to make it a valuable addition to a winning essay. There's no sizzle.

The reader should never be forced to simply have to believe you. Instead, always SHOW what you're trying to convey. A trick that can help you is to perform the *Oh really, why?* test.

Let's try it.
"I consider myself a highly motivated, talented, and dedicated student". Oh really, why? Why are you talented? Is it because you can explain the theory of relativity and sound like you know what you're talking about? Or is it that you can play the flute and juggle three oranges all at the same time? Please tell the reader why.

"...I discovered the magical results that one can achieve with a little sacrifice and hard work". Oh really, why? Did you just roll out of bed one morning and discovered this? Show the reader how.

You get the idea.

Always support your claim or statement with a clear example. Granted, the writer might have elaborated on these points in other sections of his essay. But if he has, then why even use the sentence that refers to the magical results? It becomes completely useless. Paragraphs in your body paragraph structure should flow naturally and logically throughout your essay. This is called **transitioning**. If you've already described, or are about to describe, a noteworthy talent of yours, then why would you TELL me in another sentence or paragraph how "highly talented" and "highly motivated" you are? Don't tell me if you've already shown me.

Can you identify any other writing flaws in our TELL paragraph?

Here they are:

Excessive use of I – The overuse of the I pronoun when starting a sentence can be detrimental to your essay. You can easily avoid it with a minor word pattern rearrangement. For example, you could replace *"I always work hard to keep my grades up..."*, with something like: *"Working hard to keep my grades up is a priority with me."*

Lack of details in your essay – Without details your essay becomes vague and dull. There's only so much abstract writing a reader can take. For a college essay to be successful you'll need to provide specifics. For example, it's much better to say *"I leaned out my bedroom window from our two-story house in Cleveland, Ohio"* than it is to say *"I leaned out my bedroom window."* Also, the use of details and illustrations gives the writer a chance to use imagery with their prose.

> *Clarification Note* – if you recall in one of our earlier examples, I told you not to clutter your essay with too many details. So if you're thinking I'm contradicting myself, please note that this is the difference: if you write *"I leaned out my bedroom window from our two-story house in Cleveland, Ohio, where I lived from ages 5 to 12."*.... you would probably be

guilty of giving too many details, unless the fact that you lived there from ages 5 to 12 is key to your story and becomes relevant later in your essay. Otherwise, just mentioning Cleveland, Ohio is enough to give the reader some imagery.

Poor essay transitions – A bad transition can spell the "kiss of death" and leave your essay looking disjointed.

My next chapter deals with essay transitions in more detail.

Chapter Nine

Transitioning Between Paragraphs

Transition words and phrases are the glue that hold your paragraphs together. They provide the connections needed for your paragraphs to flow seamlessly. You also use paragraph transition words within a paragraph, to account for a passage of time. Let's try injecting some transitional sentences in our SHOW example from our previous section.

While our previous example was a good paragraph, it was missing some important elements. Here's the original paragraph again:

> *"Runners take your marks," shouts the starter. My heart begins pounding hard, as I crouch down, rub my sweaty hands together, and plant my fingertips on the white line of the pavement. "Get set," yells the man with the gun. My hips shoot up. A burst of excitement fills my body. My knee is scarred and my shin is bruised from all those practice drills and long*

hours of hard training, but my will and determina-tion is stronger than ever. I am ready!

"Boom" blasts the gun. As I explode down the lane and approach the first hurdle, I think back to a time when I didn't believe in myself. A time when I didn't understand the value of personal sacrifice and hard work. And now here I am on my way to the finish line. I don't know if I'll be the first one to cross it or not, but it doesn't matter. I'm still excited. Because now I can close my eyes and picture myself crossing any finish line I may face in life."

First, the line – *"... I didn't understand the value of personal sacrifice, dedication, and hard work."* - might not withstand the "Oh really, why?" test.

Second, the transition words - *"And now here I am on my way to the finish line..."* - are carrying a heavy load. Like a time capsule, it's transitioning the reader from the past to the present, but unless you can explain how this transformation took place with a supporting sentence or in a supporting paragraph, this transition sentence doesn't hold on its own merit.

Here's the way the essay and its connecting paragraphs were originally written as part of this candidate's personal state-ment. The student's unique experience and situation gave him all he needed to explain the "why?" and transport us through his story:

"Runners take your marks," shouts the starter. My heart begins pounding hard, as I crouch down, rub my sweaty hands together, and plant my fingertips on the white line of the pavement. "Get set," yells the man with the gun. My hips shoot up. A burst of excitement fills my body. My knee is scarred and my shin is bruised from all those practice drills and long hours of hard training, but my will and determination is stronger than ever. I am ready!

"Boom" blasts the gun. As I explode down the lane and approach the first hurdle, I think back on that once shy, undersized kid that lacked self-confidence and motivation. Thank goodness my coach had the experience and patience to help me evolve. "There's a winner somewhere inside of you," he would say. "We just need to wake him up. First, you have to dare to imagine." He taught me to dream; to envision myself winning, and picture the finish line as just another hurdle in my way. We started by setting attainable goals with simple drills to build my confidence, and then working our way up to more challenging ones.

It wasn't easy. It took sweat and tears. I contemplated quitting more than once. But the dream coach planted in my head kept me going. Now here I am about to cross the finish line with no one else in front.

I've taken first place on the last five meters!

Grasping for air I turn to my coach. "Welcome home!" he shouts with a huge grin on his face as he hugs me. I feel every muscle in my body shiver with emotion. It is a feeling that I had never felt before. It's funny how something as simple as crossing a finish line can become such a defining moment. I won't take first place again for the remainder of the season, but that one experience will last me a lifetime. It taught me that with some work and sacrifice, I can close my eyes and picture myself crossing every finish line I face in life, no matter how many hurdles get in my way.

Remember – always reflect back on your own personal feelings and experiences. Then relate it in a story.

***

Here are some important "don'ts" to keep in mind as you work through your paragraph transition wording:

- **Don't** ignore the importance of a good transition. Transition statements such as "Since I've grown...", or "Ever since fifth grade..", keeps the reader on track, and helps progress the idea.

- **Don't** use passive voice verbs when you can express the same idea in an active voice. For example, say "My teacher helped me", not "I was helped by my teacher."

- **Don't** fall into the trap of the I...I...I... repetition.

- **Don't** ignore the use of imagery. As long as it's clear, it will liven up your essay.

Once you've worked on developing your story and using transition words and phrases, it's time to head for your finish line with the essay conclusion.

Chapter Ten

The Conclusion Paragraph

Don't underestimate the importance of a good conclusion paragraph for your essay. If you recall earlier in chapter five, I stressed the important role the opening paragraph plays and defined it as a critical part of your essay. The second most important part is finishing strong with good concluding sentences. The conclusion paragraph is your final chance to persuade the admissions officer and leave a lasting impression.

The Conclusion Paragraph Provides Closure
Never use your essay conclusion to introduce brand new ideas that are going generate questions or require additional explanation. Instead, use words to conclude an essay that provide closure, while sticking with your original essay theme and maintaining the same tone and voice you've had throughout the entire essay.

Avoid using stock words or phrases such as: In summary... Therefore... In conclusion... In short... etc. in your conclusion paragraph. These type of leading phrases are for formal writing. They're not really going to help your essay.

As you approach the conclusion, consider using <u>one</u> of these three techniques to end your essay:

1. **Positive Note**
   End your essay on a POSITIVE note. Whether you chose to write a soul-wrenching essay on dealing with the loss of a loved one, or a more light-hearted entertaining essay on a frustrating trip to Disneyland, end it with a positive outlook. Show the sunny side of things. Remember, the admissions staff wants to see how you make lemonade from "life's lemons."

2. **Broader Implications**
   End your essay by expanding on the broader aspects of your discussion. In other words, look at the larger picture. If your subject or discussion hints at having a more widespread appeal, make sure to work it into your essay, and particularly in the conclusion.
   For example:
   "As I was called for dinner, I couldn't believe two hours had gone by. The book was so consuming, I completely lost track of time and found myself gulping my dinner down just to get back and read more on the fascinating customs of these New Guinea aborigines. The book made me realize that while different cultures have very different conceptions of right and wrong, we're all still people and have the same problems all over the world."

1. **Full Circle**

End your essay by coming full circle. Think of your essay as a story within two "bookends." The opening paragraph is one bookend, the closing paragraph is the other.

For example:

Do you recall our earlier example of this opening paragraph from chapter five: *"Roses make a wonderful addition to my grandmother's garden, but they need a lot of water. Sometimes I feel like a rose, soaking up the world around me, eager to flourish and bloom."*

The writer might now consider for her last paragraph making some sort of connection – even if subtle – to her opening statement: *"......and I hope someday to make a positive impact in this world, just like the beautiful roses in my grandmother's garden."*

Here are some important "do's" and "don'ts" to keep in mind as you work through your concluding paragraph:

- **DO** use the final sentences to wrap up and end any suspense or answer any question that you might have posed earlier in the essay.

- **DON'T** address the admissions officer or ask them to admit you. Believe it or not, some people do this.

- **DO** use short, forceful sentences to end your essay.

- **DON'T** repeat or sum up your essay in any way. This is not a speech.

- **DO** provide closure to your essay. Use one of the methods explained above.

- **DON'T** end your essay with a quotation.

Chapter Eleven

Finish and Review Your Essay

Congratulations, you are almost there! But as you head into the final stretch, there's still one more task at hand. You now need to follow this complete checklist to review your admission essay for grammar, style and commonly misused words.

Read your essay out loud to make sure it flows well and sounds conversational. Better yet, have someone else read it out loud to you.

Use this checklist for your final essay review:

- Is your opening paragraph interesting? Does it grab the reader's attention? Is it either personal or intriguing, or does it have action or imagery?

- Is your writing friendly and personal? Or does it sound uptight and stiff?

- Have you used an active voice?

- Does your essay SHOW rather than TELL?

- Did you support your points with examples and specifics? Or is your essay full of generalities?

- Does each paragraph follow the thought you introduced in the first sentence of the paragraph?

- Check that your basic English grammatical essentials are in order (see chapter 12 and 13).

- Also check that you didn't misuse some of the most commonly confused terms (see chapter 12 and 13).

- If you're using dialogue, is it free flowing? Check your essay to see if it sounds stiff. If it does, rewrite your dialogue lines and make sure you're using contractions.

- Make sure that you haven't abused the use of adverbs and adjectives. Replace any words you would not normally use in a conversation. You don't want your essay to look like you wrote it right from a thesaurus.

- Don't write just to fill up space. Make every word and every sentence counts, and make sure every sentence moves your story forward, by describing a person, a place, a situation, or by letting the reader "hear" your voice.

- Is your essay full of clichés?

- Is your essay interesting or is it boring? Remember, if it feels boring to you it'll feel boring to the reader.

- Does your college essay end on an upbeat tone? Does it accentuate your strengths? By the end of the essay will the reader have a favorable opinion of you and like you?

- If you used dialogue, did you place periods, commas, exclamation points and questions marks inside the quotations?

- Did you use capitalization correctly?

Check your essay with this checklist above and make sure to proofread your essay. Be sure it's impeccable in form and style. It would be a shame to have it rejected after working so hard on it simply because it's full of grammatical errors, when it might have otherwise been an exceptional essay.

Final Thoughts

Avoid trying to summarize your entire essay with your last paragraph. A college admission essay is not a term paper, nor is it a like delivering a speech. In a typical speech, there is a three-part standard format: first the speaker tells the audience what he's going to be talking about; then he talks about it; then he summarizes everything he said. If you find your essay headed in this direction, rewrite the conclusion.

Don't expect to have the perfect essay after only your first draft. In case you're not aware, whether you're writing a college application essay or the great American novel, there are three rules all writers must abide by: Revise, Revise, and Revise!

Chapter Twelve

Commonly Misused Words

There are many misused words in the English language. Some have been misused words for so long, that they begin to sound right. But they are NOT. They may sound alike and might be spelled similarly, but they mean very different things. Since your admissions officer is likely well aware of them, you should be too.

Here are some of the most commonly misused phrases and confused terms together with an example of how to use them properly. Review this list and make sure you didn't misuse any of these terms in your own essay.

accede—> to agree
exceed—> to surpass

By acceding to my request he truly exceeded my expectations.

accept—> to receive
except—> excluding

I can accept any excuse except the one you just gave me.

adapt—> to receive
adopt—> to take as one's own, or formally accept

To adapt to a changing business environment, the company will adopt new measures.

adverse —> unfavorable
averse —> to be opposed

I'm averse to sleeping outdoors, especially in such adverse weather conditions.

affect —> to influence
effect —> (v)to bring about, / (n)result

Her leg injury affected her times, but it's uncertain what effect it'll have on her overall performance.

aid —> to help
aides —> staff member

The President's aides came to our aid.

all ready —> prepared
already —> previously

I am already dressed, and now I am all ready for breakfast.

allusion —> to reference
illusion —> false image
delusion —> false belief

The coach alluded to Joe's lack of effort. At first, he had illusions about Joe's level of talent and commitment, but now he's under no delusion that Joe can make any meaningful contribution to the team.

ascent —> to rise
assent —> to consent

Now that she's on her ascent to stardom, she would never give her assent to perform in a low budget film.

appraise —> to set monetary value
apprise —> to inform

I apprised her of how important it is that she have her home appraised correctly.

between —> used when two people/things are involved
among —> used when more than two people/things are involved

There are no bad feelings between you and me, but there is a lot of resentment among the rest of the group.

EXCEPTION: You may use between if each element is considered individually in relation to all the others.
There was an agreement reached between John, Sue, and Mary.

bi —> means every two
semi —> means half

It's better to get paid semimonthly, in other words, twice a month, rather than bimonthly, which is every two months.

complement —> to complete
compliment —> to praise

"Mary, your shoes are a nice complement to your dress." "Thank you, Janet." "That's a nice compliment."

continual —> repeated
continuous —> uninterrupted

John, who continually goes to the library for his research, is the kind of eager student who is continuously searching for the truth.

council —> a group
counsel —> (v) to advise, (n) advice (also used for a lawyer taking part in a court case)

The council was counseled on the potential dangers of any more budget cuts.

convince —> win over by argument
persuade —> win over by appeal to reason or feeling

It took a lot of persuasion to convince the school board of the advantages of building a new gym.

literally —> means truly
figuratively —> not the actual meaning, but a more imaginative meaning

The party last night was a "massacre" (massacre used in a figurative sense).

The American Indians were often massacred during the white man's expansion to the west (massacre used here literally).

disinterested —> impartial
uninterested —> not interested in / apathetic

I may be a disinterested observer, but I'm certainly not uninterested in the school's affairs.

e.g. —> means: for example
i.e. —> means: that is, and is used to clarify something that preceded it

I love bright colors, e.g., canary yellow or fire truck red; my sister, on the other hand, prefers softer tones, i.e. pastel colors.

elicit —> to draw out
illicit —> illegal

The mayor was able to elicit the support of the public in his fight against illicit drugs.

eminent —> prominent / respected / famous
imminent —> in the immediate future

Many eminent environmentalists feel that global warming is an imminent disaster that looms over us.

farther —> refers to physical distance
further —> refers to degree or intent

As we kept walking farther away from the camp, we discussed in further detail our plans for that evening.

fewer —> refers to numbers
less —> refers to amount

I eat fewer donuts and less ice cream than I used to.

flaunt —> to show off
flout —> to defy

He flaunted his new sports car, while he flouted the law by exceeding the speed limit.

imply —> to suggest
infer —> to deduce from available evidence or information

I infer from the expression on your face that you are implying (that) my cooking is horrible.

its —> possessive
it's —> contraction for it is

It's the largest house on its block.

ingenious —> clever
ingenuous —> naive

Sam is so ingenious he can build a tent from a few pieces of wood, and yet he can be so ingenuous he would ask a complete stranger to look after his tools.

lay —> to put something down (carefully or for a purpose) in a flat position: lay (laying), laid, laid.
lie —> to get into a horizontal position / or something that is in a particular place or position: Lie (lying), lay, laid.

I enjoy lying in bed and reading in the afternoons. I usually prepare a cup of tea first and lay it on the nightstand beside me. Yesterday, I laid in bed and read for three hours. When I was done reading, I laid my book next to my cup of tea.

loose —> unattached
lose —> to no longer possess something / misplace: (lose, lost, lost)

I lost my car keys. I had them in my pocket, but somehow they got loose. Oh well, at least I didn't lose my spare one.

precede—> to go before something or someone
proceed —> to begin or continue

It may help if you were to precede the report with an introduction, and then you can proceed with your presentation.

principal —> leader or top person
principle —> a rule

The school principal kept his word; after all, he's a man of principle.

sight —> something seen
site —> a place
sigh —> breathe out slowly and noisily, expressing some emotion

"All those flowers in the annual flower show must have been a beautiful sight to see," she sighed. "I wonder what site they'll use for next year's show."

stationary —> fixed
stationery —> supplies needed for writing

I was on my way to buy some stationery, when suddenly the traffic came to a halt and became stationary.

their —> possessive

there —> adverb that shows location

they're —>contraction for "they are"

They're going to paint every room in their house if there is enough paint.

whose —> possessive

who's —> contraction of "who is"

Who's the designated driver? I hope it's not the same person whose car just broke.

your —> possessive

you're —> contraction of "you are"

You're much better looking in person than on your driver's license picture.

Chapter Thirteen

Avoid These Expressions in Your Essay

Always avoid using inconsequential expressions in your personal essay.

Though they may seem tempting to use, they are more suited for business writing and not for a college essay. They will only serve to clutter your sentences, while making your essay less enjoyable to read.

As a result of – REPLACE WITH = Because
At the present time – REPLACE WITH = Now
At this point in time – REPLACE WITH = Now
As of this date – REPLACE WITH = Now
At that point in time – REPLACE WITH = Then
At which time – REPLACE WITH = When or During
By virtue of the fact – REPLACE WITH = Because

Come to a decision as to – REPLACE WITH = Decide

During the time that – REPLACE WITH = While

Exhibit a tendency to – REPLACE WITH = Tend to

Give consideration to – REPLACE WITH = Consider

In the event that – REPLACE WITH =If

It is often the case that – REPLACE WITH =Often

In spite of the fact that – REPLACE WITH =Although

Is of the opinion – REPLACE WITH = Believes

Pertaining to – REPLACE WITH =About

Reach the conclusion that – REPLACE WITH = Decide

The question as to whether – REPLACE WITH = Whether

This is a subject that – REPLACE WITH = This subject

Whether or not – REPLACE WITH = Whether

With reference to - REPLACE WITH = About

Chapter Fourteen

Adjectives

This list of adjectives for essay writing ideas is known as the atomic expansion effect. Start by identifying a few adjectives that might describe you best. Then brainstorm and build a theme around them. Don't be surprised if one simple premise ends up morphing into ten different story ideas!

academic – accommodating - adaptable – appreciative- active - analytical – assertive - articulate - adventurous -aggressive -artistic

bitter – bright - bold - brave

conservative – caring – considerate - capable – charming- clever – clumsy – cheerful – confidant – carefree – calm – competitive – conforming – critical – creative - conscientious - courteous - competent - congenial

determined – direct - diplomatic- dedicated - defiant - demanding- dependable - decisive efficient – enchanting – engaging- enigmatic – eccentric – economical – enterprising – entertaining - enthusiastic - energetic- eager- elegant - emotional – expressive - extreme

forgetful- friendly- fair -fearless- forgiving- flexible – follower- flamboyant- free - feminine

gentle – genuine- gloomy- gullible

handy - hopeful - humorous - humble - happy - helpful -honest

interesting – impatient – impulsive – insightful – imaginative – independent – innovative – impressionable – intuitive – influential – intelligent – introverted – irritable - informed - idealistic

jovial

knowledgeable – kind

loyal – loud – logical – loving – leading – levelheaded – lively – lazy – lackadaisical – liberal - lucky

mellow- mechanical - mature - misunderstood - modest - motivated- musical - maternal - methodical - masculine

nimble – naive – nervous – neat

organized – opinionated – objective – opportunistic – observant – original precise – provocative – practical – peaceful – pessimistic – persistent – playful - poetic – polite – pleasant- principled- protective – predictable – proud – punctual – privileged - productive

quiet

respected – reasonable - rebellious – realistic – rational – reflective – relaxed - reserved - reliable – resistant – respon- sible - receptive

straightforward – sociable – serious – selfish - sympathetic - sensible – supportive - sentimental - sensitive - stable - sin- cere - sophisticated – spiritual- spoiled – secure – strong – skillful – superstitious - stubborn - superior

tense – tenacious - temperamental - thorough - tactful - thoughtful - trustworthy - threatening - ticklish - tolerant

unbending – uncertain – useful – understanding - unconven- tional – unique - unlucky

valuable- vibrant- vulnerable - visionary – vocal - versatile - vindictive

witty – wise – workaholic – well-adjusted

Chapter Fifteen

Personal Essay Examples

Here are some actual college admission essay examples of students accepted to their targeted schools.

In each case, these essays tell us a simple story. The students shared a tiny slice of their lives and helped us learn about who they are. We found out a little bit about their upbringing and family life, or their values, fears and challenges. And the beauty of it is that they didn't have to TELL us, but rather they SHOWED us in their own unique way.

Each of these essays reflects a first-hand account or personal experience. When you have a personal experience that you can convey with imagery, emotion, and using fundamental techniques and writing skills as the type you learned from our tutorial, you have the ingredients for a great college essay.

All of these examples that follow are essays written in response to specific questions posed during the application process.

✳✳✳

1. Describe a meaningful or significant experience in
   your life.

'Twas the Saturday Before Christmas

As my eyes open slowly after a refreshing night's sleep, I see
a beautiful flurry of twinkling red and green lights. My nose
quickly picks up on the invigorating aroma of pine trees. My
ears hear gorgeous harmonized carols coming from the CD
player, coupled with the less pleasant sound of my dad's
thundering snore. I've become accustomed to these sights,
sounds, and smells because it's the weekend before Christmas.

For as long as I can remember, on the Saturday night before
Christmas, we hold the traditional family ritual of sleeping
under the Christmas tree. This tradition has grown into what
is almost a complete separate holiday from Christmas. A
holiday that my family has not only invented, but perfected
over time.

Christmas cannot arrive unless my two younger brothers, my
mom and dad, and our dog, "Fleabag", as my dad calls her,
pull out all the sleeping bags in our house and place them
beneath the tree, to prepare for our one night hibernation.
As a little kid this is what I imagined all families doing during
the Christmas season. It was a huge culture shock when I
learned from other classmates that I was the only one that

enjoyed this unique ritual. As the years continued to race by, the event grew into larger proportions. At first, it was suggested by my dad that we gather around the TV to watch a Christmas movie. Then my brothers added to that and insisted that we play Sorry, the board game. Who would have known this simple game would one day turn into the annual family Sorry Championship, the most prestigious award any member of this family can hold?

After the game (which I usually won), my mom would read The Night Before Christmas to the exhausted family. When we were younger, my parents would tell us that whoever fell asleep first would earn a candy cane from the tree in the morning; bribery at its finest. Now that we are older, we are all tall enough to reach the candy canes on the top ourselves, so that ritual has died out over the years. I'm thankful for that, because I never was the first to fall asleep. However, from this tradition came an even better one invented by my brothers and me that involved us taking all the candy canes, and placing them on the highest branches of the tree so my 5'1" mom could not reach them. I suspect that unless my mother grows three more inches this ritual will never become old.

This custom of sleeping under the tree has become a major part of my childhood. In thirty years from now, I will not remember what Santa brought me in the second grade, or how many presents I received when I was 14. What I will remember is the wonderful memories and how much I looked forward to those nights spent with my family under the beautifully decorated Christmas tree that we, as a family (mostly my father), picked out. Speaking of picking out Christmas trees, that's an entirely different tradition in itself...

***

2. Describe someone who has been big influence in your life.

Jill

"This is RED," whispered Mrs. Evelyn, my kindhearted kindergarten teacher, as she pointed to a crayon on her desk. "RED," my young sheepish voice repeated back. Coming from Argentina and settling in a suburb of New York, my parents had become part of a long legion of immigrants that gave up their home to come to the land of opportunity. As a five-year-old boy unfamiliar with the English language, I found myself in a strange setting. It felt as if I were riding on a noisy merry-go-round that had no music, just loud voices that I couldn't understand. The more voices I'd hear, the faster the merry-go-round turned, and all I wanted to do was jump off.

To ease my language-learning process, Mrs. Evelyn teamed me up with a student named Jimmy. Jimmy was lots of fun, but he was a spirited freckled-faced boy who seemed to be lacking in the pedagogical skills department. Indeed, he was more interested in sneaking up behind Tommy and knocking his blocks down, or pulling on Mary's pigtails, rather than spending his time on English lessons. I can't say I blamed him. Realizing things weren't working out with Jimmy, Mrs. Evelyn teamed me up with Bobby instead. Unfortunately, Bobby left for another school early in the year. So Mrs. Evelyn turned to yet a third student. Her name was Jill.

"A girl?" I thought to myself. "This can't be!" My fragile male ego was mortified. At that moment I hated my parents for ever dragging me into this country. Jill wasted no time and quickly got to work. She grabbed me by the hand and walked me through the classroom. She would point out at various objects, and I would grudgingly repeat her words: "chair," "wall," "blackboard," and so on. I couldn't help feeling like a caged parrot. Jill was relentless. In her heart, she believed she was serving a worthy cause and it showed. In fact, she went far and beyond the call of duty. One day a first grade bully approached me in the hallway. With a motherly instinct and a stern look, she stepped between us as if she were a screen keeping away some annoying bug.

Pretty soon, I began soaking up this new vocabulary like a dry sponge soaking up water. I found myself looking forward to each new school day, and I particularly enjoyed the company of this skinny, blond-headed girl with an angelic face. After a while, I was the one doing all the pointing and leading the way, eager to learn new words, as Jill followed me and responded to every question with a grin on her face. As the days turned into weeks, and the weeks turned into months, all the voices and the talking I would hear around me began to finally make sense. Suddenly, there was music in my merry-go-round!

With the passage of time and successive school years, I lost track of Jill. I'm sure, though, wherever she may be, that she's probably bringing joy to someone's life and making it a little better. As for me, my newly acquired language skills paved the way for a lifetime of friends and memories, plenty of academic achievements, future college plans, and even what I hope someday will turn out to be a rewarding career in journalism. And while Jill may not be responsible for all of this, she can at least take credit for part of it, and be certain she'll always have a warm place in my heart.

3. Write a personally satisfying experience.
(no title)

Cowabunga! Cowabunga!" This was the battle cry I heard from my two younger brothers early every Saturday morning. "Come on Adam, Teenage Mutant Ninja Turtles is on in five minutes!" Looking back, there's no way I could have predicted how much that cartoon series would influence my life. It's a good thing my brothers were so loud and persistent in waking me up on time to watch it. As we crowded around the TV set at our California home, we agonized with each week's episode watching our heroes step into danger, and then cheered ecstatically as we witnessed them ultimately triumph over evil.

The Turtles always stood up for each other against the evil Shredder, but only working together were they able to defeat him. This Saturday morning cartoon was the glue that bonded us together. While other siblings in our neighborhood fought constantly with each other, we took the Turtles as models and realized that being brothers meant being part of a team. We felt fortunate to be brothers. The fascination with the Turtles led us to create and play our own imaginary games together. There was no time for playing video games alone in our rooms. Sensing this was more than just a passing fad in our lives, my parents searched for a martial arts studio suitable for a six-year old Turtle enthusiast, and his two younger brothers.

Within a week, we began taking Tae Kwon Do classes together. It was shocking for us to see other kids making fun of their brothers and sisters when they made mistakes, because this is something the Turtles would never do. For the next several years we attended the studio looking forward to each and every session. We supported each other, and on occasion even competed against each other. As we grew older, the Turtles quietly withdrew from the center stage of our lives, to become more and more just a peripheral part of our existence. But their magic never really left our spirit. It was with this team spirit that we accomplished what many around us would never accomplish; we all reached the rank of black belt at a young age. For most people, "Teenage Mutant Ninja Turtles" represents just another product of our pop culture; a cartoon created for commercial purposes, with characters that made a good Halloween costume.

For me, however, they will always mean much more than that. These Turtles edged a path that brought me closer to my brothers. They introduced me to the martial arts, which ultimately taught me confidence, discipline, and respect for others. To this day, I'm close and supportive of my brothers, and I continue my training in Tae Kwon Do. All thanks to four mutated Turtles that fought evil every Saturday morning.

***

4. Write a personally satisfying experience (same question as #3)

The Longest Ten Seconds

After a long physics test on a sweltering summer day, I felt exhausted. I was on my way out of the classroom, when Mr. Fang found me. "Hi, Jane, can you come with me now? It's something important and I think you'll like it." I was confused, but politely smiled back and followed him. "What on earth are we going to do?" I wondered.

He stopped and went into the auditorium, as I followed right behind. To my surprise, the huge auditorium was full of people: students, teachers, foreign teachers, the principal, vice principals, and counselors. "Something must be going on here", I thought as I felt the excitement and energy of the room fill my body. It even made me forget about how tired and hungry I was. I found an empty seat at the back, forgetting all about Mr. Fang's words. Soon I realized that it was actually an English improvisational speech contest to select top orators to go to nationals. This was without a doubt a great opportunity for English learning.

Nine 12th graders went up one by one to deliver their speeches. The topics were randomly chosen so that they couldn't prepare ahead of time. After the ninth candidate completed his speech, the whole auditorium became quiet. Then Mr. Fang stood up. He looked around as if he was searching for someone. My heart was pounding hard. What am I worrying about? No way. I'm only in the 10th grade. But when Mr. Fang made eye contact with me and waved me on to the front of the auditorium, I realized my fears were not unfounded.

"Mr. Fang, what do I need to do?" I asked. My hands were sweaty, and my throat was dry. "Draw a topic, prepare for three minutes and deliver your speech," he answered. "I had decided to let you participate this afternoon," he said. "But I couldn't reach you because of your physics test. I'm sorry about that, but I think you'll do fine." I took a deep breath, and my brain started to work faster and faster. "Calm down. Be confident. You love challenges, don't you?" I said to myself. As I looked around, I felt comfort and reassurance seeing the smiles on my teachers' faces. Suddenly, a surge of courage and confidence rushed through my body. I was excited, and surprisingly felt at ease in front of this large audience.

The topic I drew was about my opinion on the reform of the Chinese educational system, specifically the college entrance examination. It was not an easy one, but lucky for me it was one I was familiar with, since my multicultural educational experiences provided me some strong supportive evidence for my opinion. I went to the stage, stood up straight, and began my first improvisational speech. The further into the speech I got, the more relaxed I felt. I lost track of time as the words kept pouring out of my mouth.

When I ended my speech, there was an unnerving moment of silence. Within two seconds my face turned red as a ripe apple, and my heart was ready to burst out of my chest. Though the silence only lasted about five seconds, it seemed like a century to me. Then I heard a thundering applause. It was such a huge relief! Those five seconds felt like the longest of my life. I went from extreme anxiety to overwhelming happiness. It was an amazing and joyful moment. I looked at Mr. Fang, and he was smiling at me as always, but more proudly, more happily.

About the Author

I'm an award-winning columnist, author, editor and teacher, who has dedicated a lifetime to the wonderful art of making writing fun. My writings appear in a variety of publications, including *Boys' Life, Christian Home and School, Readers' Digest, Chicken Soup for the Soul,* and *Christian Science Monitor,* as well as in many state standardized testing books, including *Measuring Up to the New York State Learning Standards,* and *Measuring Up to the Texas Essential Knowledge and Skills,* among others.

During these wonderful years I've had the pleasure of raising three young boys who have also attended college, and who have since grown into fine young men.

If you've enjoyed this guidebook please consider posting a review. I'm always happy to hear your comments and suggestions.

Click here or scan the QR code below to leave your honest review.

SCAN HERE!

Made in the USA
Coppell, TX
15 June 2024

33553814R00056